MARRA · FAMILIA

William Martin was born in 1925 in Silksworth, Co. Durham, and now lives in Sunderland. His first two collections *Cracknrigg* (1983) and *Hinny Beata* (1987) were published by Taxus Press. *Marra Familia* (Bloodaxe Books, 1993) is his third book of poems.

MARRA · FAMILIA
WILLIAM · MARTIN
What · KINGDOM · Without
COMMON · FEASTING

BLOODAXE BOOKS

ISBN: 1 85224 221 3

First published 1993 by
Bloodaxe Books Ltd,
P.O. Box 1SN,
Newcastle upon Tyne NE99 1SN.

Bloodaxe Books Ltd acknowledges
the financial assistance of Northern Arts.

ACKNOWLEDGEMENTS
Anna Navis was first published by *The Page* (Northern Echo); an extract
was published in *High on the Walls: a Morden Tower Anthology* (1990).
Part of *Triptych* was broadcast on Tyne Tees Television's *Elements*.
Many thanks to my dear wife Win for her loving help always,
and to Gordon Brown for his support over the years.

Cover printing by J. Thomson Colour Printers Ltd, Glasgow.

Printed in Great Britain by
Cromwell Press Ltd, Broughton Gifford, Melksham, Wiltshire.

To my grandchildren
Georgia Elizabeth
Stephanie Ann
Rachel

...here's a rush to light you to bed
here's a fleece to cover your head
against the world-storm
brother by sister
under one brethyn
kith of the kin warmed at the one hearth-flame...

DAVID JONES
The Tutelar of the Place

CONTENTS

 SHARD

(Paleapaphos)

I roll paste-eggs
On her ruined mosaic floor

Easter rain washes away veils

The great stone
Proud with oils
Uncovered for all to see

They come from the sea to be born

They eat stained eggs
Crackling open

ⲅⲁⲣ ⲙ̄ⲙⲁⲧ
ⲛ̄ⲧⲟⲩ ⲛ̄ϣⲏⲛ
ϩⲙ̄ ⲡⲁⲣⲁ'ⲇⲓⲥⲟⲥ ⲉⲥⲉⲕⲓⲙ
ⲁⲛ ⲛ̄ϣⲱⲙ' ⲙ̄ⲡⲣⲱ
ⲁⲩⲱ ⲙⲁⲣⲉⲛⲟⲩⲱⲃⲉ
ϩⲉ ⲉⲃⲟⲗ
ⲡⲉⲧ·

 # SHARD

Version of an Irish poem

Twice she came
The maiden with great longing
She left my cheek pale
And furrowed my brow with care

Twice she came
And she will come again
For she is a Mazer
A wonderful one
And I still wait there

AVE·BEATA

AKR·EENY·MEENY·MACKER·RACKER·RARE·O·DOMMIN·

1.

Ave Beata eyes close
On fossil Mothergate

Safety-light flickers in coiled black

Kingdom escapement triggered

Governor eye-lids
Closing and closing

(As lang as aa live aall nivvor forget)

Her after-image pink

2.

Ave Beata in tears to her brim

Floodgate out of condensed black

Two by two droplets
Fetch storm waves

Black and white dove
With a Jesse branch grafted

Semen buds crying

Droplets rocking the Ark

3.

Ave Beata not a single tongue

All tongues in tower

Split tip speaks to her
From babble at gate entry

Collective interpretation going on

(Wor Nanny's a Mazer)

Incarnation fleshed

4.

Ave Beata my touch is a real touch

Not light on her curve
Teaching eyes cast out

Or hand lost in thought
The evil plucked bodyless

Real Ave Beata
Her Marradharma
All hand-senses reach

(And a Mazer she'll remain)

 SONG

Lady will you come with me
To the starry land
To the marvellous land
Lady will you come with me
To the starry marvellous land

No one speaks of property
In that speckled-egg land
In that glittering band
No one speaks of property
In that speckled-egg glittering band

Lady will you come
You'll wear a golden crown
Milk and honey we'll share
In that faraway whispered of land..
Lady will you come
You'll wear a golden crown
Milk and honey we'll share
In that faraway
Whispered of land

IMAGE · ARK

1.

My coble
Slips on
Shell sand

Oystercatchers shift

Sun-colour
Their bills rising

As morning
Squeaks in
Across water

2.

Rising and falling
My bow cuts horizon

The sun's blood
A slick dispersing

It turns into gold
It turns to silver sparkle

Seals howl out of dark
To bottle a message

3.

Spouted message
In coded words
Wriggles out of helm

Characteristic handy-work on them

An upright heron
Alone in wrack-field
Waits to beak

4.

Black cliffs spoiled white
Stink on either side

Blue-white coble
Pointed between

Caller-fresh fish
Brought to each bedside table

Morning star
With chorus
Last to be seen

5. (Virgin of the Rocks
Bay of Kotor Montenegro)

Lady of Rocks
In your white silvered sheet

Head only uncovered

My hand is still rowing
This coble engraved
Whirlpool around you

Lady of rocks
Come out of destruction

Lady of rocks
They thorn you in roses

6

Sand banks the haven rock
Stiff fulmar turns around

I wait for your call
In the morning

Glad Tidings ready
Wind drifting me from shore

The sun is up and going
Proud noon coming

7. SONG

Out of the haven
The bonny morning went

A wake now across water
The magic moment spent

Ripples at the sea's edge
Lapped low light farewell

Folk at the haven-house
Were ringing the morning bell

8.

I am riding
The fetch waves

Leaving morning
On their tips

When rising breezes
Cast off the froth early

Time ringing sea bells
On my sharp coble pointer

9.

But where is the figurehead
Fit for this prow

The capped dark lady
Bursting at seams

Her belly-fire
Raked down on us

Her banners in flame-light
For night and day shifters

10.

She opened herself to us
In Eden forests where she lay

We were hand in hand walking then
Like the first day forever

Flood came and went
With the moon-ark still sailing

Two by two
In and out
Where she lay

11.

Fossil-rings
Say things
Year after year

Black words hidden
Pressed under clay

Harvey and Hutton
A heat-pyre banked up

Swamp-logs
Fallen on her
Where she lay
Under Kabbala

12.

She lay on Malkuth rooted

Gripping earth-brood
To Kingdom

Tapping selection juices

Redeeming market-like forces

Handing down
A fossil crown

13.

Children hop hitchydabber
On her pavement Kabbala

They pitch their tin dabber
Hop up the dark tree

'Who'll bring the crown down
For Magdalene Mary

Under lamp-light
Under star-light

Who'll bring it for me'

14. SONG

O hinny bird hinny bird
Turn in your bed

O hinny O hinny
Turn round your head

Green gravel green gravel
The grass is so green

The bonniest lass
That ever was seen

15.

Here's a lass
With a bright thole pin

Here are the sailors
Sailing in

Here's a shepherd
Come to sing

Early in the morning

16.

Ikthus fisherman
Kissed her head

He touched her eyes
In her dreamer bed

Littoral gospeller
Saw her wed

Quite early in the swell

17.

They stood in shooting green
Early in the morning

They stood in high gold corn
Early in the day

They walked in stooked fields
Blessed are the meek ones

They gathered her cradle straw
Blessed is the day

18.

Here comes the lass
With her bright thole pin

Here come the sailors
To carry her in

A lone shepherd waits ashore
Longing to sing

Early in the morning

19. SONG

Wash her in milk
And dress her in silk

And write down her name
With a gold pen and ink

O hinny O hinny
Turn round your head

Hinny bird hinny bird
Turn round your head

20.

Steady amber light
And flashes either side

Curved apogee nightfall
And coming moon-way pick-up

Her pilot
Undeviating
In later
Cloud-race
Appearing

21.

Summon the stars
To navigate

Touch sails
To cold air

Turn away
From red lights alarming

Go for green
Between wet
Shifting
Underwater grit

22.

My Lady of Kazan
I came a long way
To your homeland

Three times named
I came to your special place

Where new beginning soured
And common things
Were commandered
For nothing

23.

I remember the spring banners
Fresh in wind beating

Dust and loose attachments
All gone away

Vivid colour licked new
The idea relevant again

Her gift
Always accessable
Sufficient

24.

How is her day
To be ordered
After sailing

Her farmer knows well
The colour of going...

Are all our days
Thought of then

Bindings laid bare
When the silver boat beaches

25.

Sun and fool's gold
On ocean skin stretching

It lays over deeps
Outer-light hardly reaching

Wrecks of remembrance
In mind out of sight

Recollection through gold
Tempting reflection

26.

Canny to me
It seemed
On our sailing

Down the sea lane
Along the dark lonnen

Land ahoy daily
Lost in
Gull noise
Each morning

Words from her hailer
Massed birds fight over

27.

Only the word
Only the word

Out of her substance
Causing disorder

Over the limited ocean
Over the limited sea

Landfall a certainty
Words washed ashore

28.

Stars boundless
Yet bound to us

Guide our puny
Or momentous undertaking

Plucked fruit they seem
Plucked or about to be

Their ways are our ways
Which way the moon sails

29. SONG

Three cobles are coming
From out the deep sea
Three cobles are coming
For Elsie and me
Who'll stand in the black prow
Leading them inshore
Three cobles are coming
So sing once more sing

Three cobles are coming
With spices and gold
Coming for children
Out in the cold
Three cobles are coming
Decked red black and white
She'll stand in the black prow
Last night or tonight

30.

The swirling look-out flashes
Its green eye watches forward

Pilot on board (carefully)
Islands all the way in

Shore voices mouthless (hidden)

Misunderstood tongues
Wagging forest logos

31.

Five trees in Paradise...

But I do not hear
The Kingdom wind
Stirring their branches and twigs

Five trees in Paradise
Even in winter wind
From the North Sea
Or summer gusts against blue
With children jumping in it
Their coats held out

No stirring even then
And their leaves do not fall

32.

Askr and Embla
Becker and Ock
And Pin straight
Up to the sky

These are the five trees Paradise

They have waited a long time
Their fruit held in limbo

Not frozen but juicy
Ready to eat
Seed set to fly

33.

I am in the wind
Reaching them

It is 'how' that the wind says

Emphasis turbulance
Touching their ear-shot

Shaking out parasites
Testing each root grip

Trying to trying
Sub-senses awaken

34.

How long can I sing
The old song each morning

Red like the shepherd
Her hands raised to greet me

She spoke the words twice
And I sing in their spirit

Ship on the wind
Will it carry me with them

 SONG

Up the leafy lonnen
With windows green as grass
Call at my hinny's door
She's a bonny lass
With roses in her bosom
With pollen on her chin
Knock at the door and lift her latch
Come in my hinnies come in

Tread the path the black path
Of dust to dusty duff
Come down 'in first' my hinnies
Walk along with us
We'll hide their pipe and baccy pouch
We'll hide them under thorn
Come down my hinnies
Walk with us 'the morn'

Is this the way to Bethlehem
It seems so very far
Is this the colour of Bethlehem
Riding on a star
Come sing of the golden river
Sing of the silver boat
If this is the way to Bethlehem
This is the way we'll go

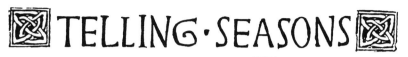

TELLING · SEASONS

DECEMBER · MARCH

JVNE · SEPTEMBER

DREAMTIME

1.

Roll the sun
Out of the sea
When my keel goes

Blow the wave tips
To carry it in

Boil the surf breakers
And lift the sun ladle

Dazzle the salt pans
Once more her day bring

2.

Bend the ecliptic
A rainbow around her neck

Touch her flower dresses
Their petals wide open

Walk the track laid down
So tirelessly wear the grass

Sink in her red blood
And kiss her eyes closing

3.

Canny to me the season of telling

Sun risen in cleft hills

In solstice notch
Rocking from dark breast
To dark breast

Red knob of fire by
Ecliptic path tilted

Just awake bird noise

Red wing on nipple

4.

They write the blessed words
In pollen dust under each chin

They sing the blessed tune
In burrows and dark places
Like under a leaf

They dance the blessed hopping way
Along eyesight straight to horizon

They speak to shells
Disconnected from
Bony skull houses

5.

Canny to me the season of telling

Kingdom feet for a song raise dust

It nostrils black snot
Intrudes between toes

It reaches out trodden
Off track between hills

Wise men star bent up ahead

6.

She splayed her legs wide when the minders said

Pushing under starlight instruction

Her wisdom crown stretched
Round his mucus head
Wreath hair dressed

Slither out ravelled

Kingdom toe last to leave

Birth under harrow

Malkuth his first step

31

7.

Nights throng under stars

Canny the feet * even of them

They crush to queue there every morning

Seeking ingrained light
On intense unbelievable tiptoes

Days throng to meet somewhere
Out of sight early

Cleavage hollow aligning them

Coming solstice overturned

8.

The whole body is loose
From its Chrysalis clock

Time-out days squeezed together

Red expansion collapsing

Exponential grown backwards

Primal Adam with candles
Hauling the black stuff back
To his shoreline with fishes

9. SONG

Jack shine the Maggi
Cry Jack shine the Maggi
Follow her Jack's Maggi light
Into dark

Jack shine the light in her
Jack shine the Maggi
Shine again Jack
In the dark

10.

Black fossil path going all night
Into her secretly under lamps

She touches faces
Smudged with her fingers

Traces scattered on
Ripe corn stubble

Weight pressing roots back
Into black harvest seams

11.

Dark dreams
(Under daylight skin
Moving across fields)

Broken on the morn's morn

The Caller's long shadow
Standing against walls

His high summer boots sounding
In her Blind Lane dazzled

12.

Don't sleep the Caller
Drawn in your slumber

Don't sleep the Caller
Endlessly rocking there

Don't sleep the Caller
He's knocking each chalked up time

Don't sleep the Caller
His first shift will ride

13.

Law at the highest point
Hauls Stephenson waggons
To gravity over-the-top
Full ones on incline

Jam-jar kids climb battery sides
'All eyes' for steel rope twitch

Heaped fossil-swamp passes them

In toadflax spawn
Her orange spots wriggle

14.

Lost Black Woods alongside
Lead down to Chapelgarth palings

They run past the gaps
A see-inside movement

It flicks like a film
Giving no seat for comfort

Just an after reflection
A fleeting retina

15. SONG

She shines in dark fencing
Cut up through pale gaps

Beyond partial vision
Scriptum bowl on her lap

So brightly fragmented
Hoary wares at the rim

Glory O

Glory O

Who'll sing caller in

16.

Whispers over breath
Find word condensing

Flesh its new touch
Hesitant under cover

Her hands around waist
Into copulation overcome

Out of her eyes dark possible Spring

Proud green shoots held stiff in new light

Agitated profusion

Flower-head spurt

17.

Noon equilibrium

Ash-sticky buds catch light seeds
In wind still centre turning about

Six foot branched Menorah
With imminent Maytime roots

Roots unite to summer breaking down
Combing soil after frost

Trimmed sticky wicks burn rape oil

Late ash-black opening gold

18.

Billy horns
Over the hill
Swept by west wind
All day bringing tears

Horizontal split pupils...

How long the orange
Iris takes to set

Eye-lid trees newly planted

They touch over bloodshot

It is grassed over

19.

Eggs roll on her body...
Onion stain and butter rubbed

They fill the hollow

Decorated pelvic bones
Hold them jarping

On wrap-around pathway

Old pipe stems

And crockery-shell fragments

Embedded

20.

Canny to me
The season
Of telling

Feet breaking grass

Cow-parsley haze

Spiked gorse-blaze
Shimmering light
Out of cliffs
Just uncovered
Since the ice

21.

Chill waves warm to
Yellow shaking fire

Cold stones grind us to dust

Diminishing
Years ahead
Of the moon
Drawing zig-zag

Yellow cosmic tide
Brings us back

Fire thorns on the shore

22. SONG
(sing pieces in italics)

If I were a blackbird
I'd whistle and sing

Longshore words move like
Dunlin across shifting wet

And wait for the ship
That my true love sails in

Frothing sweep erases

And on the top rigging
I'd there build my nest

Swirling flight turns another page

And pillow my head
On her lily white breast

23.

Red wings
Sip the morning
Into newness

Ancient vows whispered
To clamouring birds

Words monitored
By flower heads
Open again

Egging body-contours discovered
Fresh mind-eye hands all over

24.

Rain later
Washes her
Lying in pools

Delayed image
Reflecting blue

New blue on the day
Of his first touch

Thought
Moving old hands
On the girl
Rising to meet him

25.

West he walks

Immortality orchids
Spotted in gouged space

Sand and gravel made
Concrete somewhere

Coal waste
On limestone
Left dipping
To Copt Inn cross

Flaming feet on the way
To June ending

 SONG

Will dayligone fash
Or be egged on in fettle
Its bleezer laid idle
Claes hoyed forgetten
Will neet louse its bairn
In forst heed the caaller
In hadaway neet-time
The morn's morn's nigh hand

We'll rise up aall soakin
Like babbies out o' watter
We'll gan to her gatherin
Each one a marra
We'll tack the wide lonnen
It's nee good the narra
In hadaway neet-time
When the morn's morn's nigh hand

HOW·MANY·MILES ·:·TO·BABYLON·:·

ANNA·NAVIS

 SONG

How many miles to Babylon
Three score and ten
Can I get there by candlelight
Yes and back again
Here's a beck then and here's a boo
Open your gates and let us all through
Open your gates and let us all through

1.

Crowned heads rise early
In brass morning sun

Sleepers resurrected
Out of black earth

Steel rollers and bobbins
Smashed under hammer

Scrap-value line
Built over and ploughed

Only feet bring remembrance

2.

Black marra banners

Thump!

Sounding brass slowly

Thump! again

Climb the hill

Thump! the big drum goes

3.

Out of stars quickly fading
With Milky Way spilt

Blue at the rim
As the cat comes in

Stars leave to remember
Sky banners draped black

Lamped fathers rise
Out of pulley-wheel eyes

Bairns loaded on back

4.

It rises in cleft
On a dry reef remnant

Brass blare and drum thump
To her North Door knocker

Dawn limestone flora
Edge her worn pathway

Ghost rhyme remembrance
Worded by redundant men

Gathering for crack

5.

Shit flies grub the
Smell rejoicing

Midden men shovel
With arms-length handle

Cart on curved track tipping
Into house-stone quarry

Surrounding coiled wire rusting

Ashen ash-stained the patch

6. SONG

Pit lie idle pit lie idle

Over stiles and up the lonnen
Saw a moose run up the waall

Up the lonnen they'll be gannin
Pit lie idle O

Soon they'll gather on the beck-side
Saw its arse and that was aall

Bait and crack and idle backsides
Pit lie idle O

7.

Black marra banners

Thump!

Sounding brass slowly

Thump! again

Climb the hill

Thump! the big drum goes

8.

She heaves
Her hip shadow
Over daylight hawthorn

Green droplet tears
Evaporate
Not ready for the beak

Steam hiss on the
Hope's steep battery sides
Cloud her eyes reading the
Morning Star's last twinkle

Soon lost between lines

9.

Uncounted crownings
Sighted like starlings

July migration unperched
By her caller's knock

Silver prize bandsmen warm
Breath-horns in gathering

Winged noise grows louder
Till seven strikes down-wind

Silk banner flappings they'll follow

10.

Undreamed hollow words
Soon fill out when sleep-walking

Ink in at the foot
Their dream-stuff made

Hymn-heads first bared
Then Hail the Conquering Hero

Two hundred bands
Spoke into hub-city waiting

Shaver keen on daa's back

Curled golden words

11.

They enter a marvellous rage

Not drowned imagination
But indignation at separation

Rootless mercy gathering tears

Who's name tongues the flugel
Who's heart-beat paces drum

Who's word jingles tokens
On tubs come out of her

Black under waste-mott

12.

Here and here our Jerusalem
Is under this sun crowded

Not under unconcious collective
But all things in open bright day

Bairns touch banner hem
For power proudly winded

Our banner played
Down town-road redeemed
To candymen lost

13.

Black marra banners

Thump!

Sounding brass slowly

Thump! again

Climb the hill

Thump! the big drum goes

14.

Fellside bread brought once
To make words here

Crust-syllables syntax
Real eating for every day

Water table drinking springs
Mark scoffed lines
This noontide laid out

(Not special Sabbath words
Rumbling hungry indoors)

All tasted and shared

15.

Where is our feeding to come

The banners say know who you are
And know you must stand together

Will it come out of sky
Sun clouded with bird flight

Will it spout from the sea's edge
Shoals secretly gasping

Where is our feeding
To Tom Dick and Harry

The banners say know who you are

16.

Black marra banners

Thump!

Sounding brass slowly

Thump! again

Climb the hill

Thump! the big drum goes

17.

Dreams bump into dark

Stumble-lamp under gauze veil
Lighting her face

Pick-knowledge fragmented
Stone broken-fruit offered

A roundy on fire back
Waiting to tongue
Her spitting words
They'll hook-fashion
Into mat scroll

18.

Her carpet page
Is all over us

Each stitch
A crowned head
Under fire

Feet burnish gold
To hessian bare
Of cut rags

They roll
A new ball
And roll
A new frame

The same

19.

Flames glint hook-progger out

Steel barb-woof muffles glint in

Loop cuttings untied
Under bare foot
Out of bath

Soap slab on hearth
To scrub every inch pink

Except pulley-wheel eyes

Hauling tubs and men

Back to pit again

20.

Black marra banners

Thump!

Sounding brass slowly

Thump! again

Climb the hill

Thump! the big drum goes

21.

July trains whistle
Up a golden thread line

Past Pallion and Hylton
Only wind it all in

Through Penshaw and Sunniside
All the way into her

July trains whistle
Up a golden thread line

22.

Sooted half-grown fields
Drilled on her track sides

Half way to Dunholm
Darkening the cold green corn

Half way from seed
To golden fossil waves

Our ship steaming in

Half way to banners unfurling

Half way wind in brass

23.

They by-pass grass lovers in pollen

The dun-cow girl
Shouting a place-name

Her breasts polished yellow
His hands out of rape fields

This train awake going
And going and going there

A steamed open book
Down among gold leaf
Bold words rolled out

24.   *(sing the pieces in italics)*

'Tis the gift to be simple
'Tis the gift to be free

They will gather by the river

'Tis the gift to come down
Where we ought to be

They will gather by the river
Where we are

And when we find ourselves
In the place just right

There we shall be
With her banners and brass sounding

'Twill be in the valley
Of love and delight

25.

I come with passion
At the edge

A singer
To meet me
Of the old song
Passing all comfort

Some words
Weep me
Down to you
Bones of my bones

26.

It is not
Babylon
That remains

It knocks at her
Great North Door
Thronged with
Changeling banners
And backward reading words

Songs that sound
Like the old songs
Inside out

27.

And we come in
Through corn trembling

The hiss of seed
Tinnitus overwhelming

And we come to you hinny
With waste-land banners
And fire brands

Crackling reflections
In the dark water

SONG

How many miles to Babylon

Three score and ten

Can I get there by candlelight

Yes and back again

Here's a beck then and here's a boo

Open your gates and let us all through

Open your gates and let us all through

 SONG

By hills and bells far chiming
By hills and bells so high
Sits a downcast lady nursing
A bairn by candlelight
Deep shadows at each shoulder
Deep shadows on her head
Bent fingers holding the lapped child
Light on his head

Bairn by candlelight
Light on his head
Bent fingers holding the lapped child
Light on his head

Whisht to the bairn in candlelight
By hills and bells so high
Whispered whisht to the bairn's eyes closing
Pale lips up to downcast eyes
Deep shadows at each shoulder
Deep shadow on her head
Bent fingers holding the lapped child
Light on his head

Bairn by candlelight
Light on his head
Bent fingers holding the lapped child
Light on his head

TRIPTYCH

1. Eden Words (1–3)

The updraught is
Between reef breasts

The smell of burning
Her body celebrated

The last
Black womb-script
Raked onto fireside blather

Cold meat
And fried taities
All week and Sunday night marras

2.

Frisky gallowas
And crushed bones
Heaped under ski-slope

Twin shafts capped

Over trodden
Immobile banners
Tubs pass by the score

Cockerooso bairns
Climb bright
Mothergate frames

Fossil generations
Hop across her flame

3.

She stands in flame
Speaking black Eden words

She rakes down damping
Making green smoke
For a little while longer

She dances on fire
The blazer increasing its tempo

She touches waste
Tipped on fields
Smouldering out of her seams

4. Bonefire (4–7)

Marra O Marra
It is a strange land

We laid down
Our instruments
By the water haugh

Summer field flooded

We laid them down
Under banners
When they asked us to sing

5.

Our true picture they said

After-thought feeding
The handout mouths

Our true picture

Striving with
Jingling pocket
To win over them

Our true way leads to
A counting house vision

But I'll not be loser

Our true song
You sing our true song for us

6.

But we blew into brass

Warming labyrinthine
Song threads
Reaching out of horn

The morning sun
Glinting
On rose-window Majesty

Flags turning red
Bones set on fire

Her breath out of black
When our song came at last

7.

Like fossil coal
Under glass
Bone-box fragments

Her Malkuth engraved
At the black oak
Pieced foot end

Her child
A bright spark
Setting us alight

Bones of our bones ignited

Fathers and mothers
And sisters and brothers
In the will of us all

8. Slogan Bread (8–10)

Banner stitches hem them

Touched power encircled

Word issue
Their bait
Gathered round
High on fellside

Good crack yeast

Dough-rise on fender

Banners hem them encircled
Teeth sunk into slogan

9.

Loaf-tin words
Smell of rite eating

Where love begins
Crusts curl every hair

We are compressed
Into commonness

Food is for one mouth all over

Who feels the hunger pain?
No space between us

10.

Hands in oven-well ink
Make ripe golden words

Black fell IN PRINCIPIO
Our corn-sickle inscription

Cut green-vellum grass
And stretched
Cow parsley haze

Words broken to mouth
On a table before us

HYMN

(Sing the pieces in italics)

Wide wide as the ocean
High as the Heavens above

We stood still like ice
In the street under stars

Deep deep as the deep blue sea
Is my Saviour's love

We opened the Maggi light
Through her hawthorn crown
Close to grass

I am so unworthy
Still I'm a child of his care

We hopped across
At the final Cockerooso cry

For his word teaches me that his love reaches me

EENY MEENY MACKER RACKER RARE O DOMMIN ACKER

Everywhere

NOTES

The cross design is from the 7th century Wearmouth-Jarrow bible the Codex Amiatinus, now in Florence. The Greek-Coptic text within it is from a Gnostic work the Gospel of Thomas: 'For you have five trees in Paradise which do not stir in summer or in winter and their leaves do not fall.'

And a few words that might be unfamiliar:

Marra: Equal like kind, comrade friend workmate.

Mothergate: The main roadway in a pit.

Mazer: An amazing person.

Coble: A North-East fishing boat.

Malkuth: Hebrew, the Kingdom.

Hinny: A term of endearment possibly derived from 'honey'.

Canny: Nice, good, easy.

In first: In the first shift.

The morn: Tomorrow.

Maggi: From the children's game 'Jack shine the Maggi (or light)'. This was a most mysterious game, played in the dark. The children divided into two groups. One group went off into the dark with a torch or lantern, the purpose being to find the group with the light. When the pursuers shouted 'Jack shine the Maggi' the light had to be switched on briefly. The holders of the light then moved on and hid somewhere else. I like to think that the Maggi is derived from the Magi who followed the star.

Caller: Fresh new.

Dayligone: Daybreak.

Fash: Will not be bothered.

Fettle: In this sense meaning to be in good condition.

Pulley-wheel: Pit winding gear.

Crack: Chat, news, conversation.

Whisht: Hush be quiet.

Cockerooso: A popular game when I was a boy. One of the children stood in the middle of the road while the others gathered on one pavement. The middle kid called on one of the gathering to try to hop across the road, the aim being to prevent this by shoulder-charging. If a foot was put down that person stayed in the middle to help. If the hopper got across he or she would shout 'Cockerooso' and all the others then hopped across. After a while the game got rather boisterous as the sides were evened up.

SONGS

Lady will you come with me: My version of part of an old Irish poem. My own tune.

Out of the haven: My own words and tune.

O hinny bird and *Wash her in milk:* My own words and tune.

Three cobles: My own words and tune.

Up the leafy lonnen: My own words and tune.

Jack shine the Maggi: My own words and tune.

She shines in dark fencing: My own words. Tune 'The Bold Fenian Men'.

If I were a blackbird: Traditional words and tune.

Will dayligone fash: My own words and tune.

How many miles to Babylon: Children's verse, own tune.

Pit lie idle: Italicised words traditional, tune my own.

'Tis the gift to be simple: Shaker words and tune.

By hills and bells: My own words, tune 'Bonnie at Morn'.

Wide wide as the ocean: Hymn tune and words.

THE·END·OF
MARRA·FAMILIA
THANK·YOU·FOR
READING·THIS
WORK